No More Hiroshimas

ジェイムズ・カーカップ

ノー・モア・ヒロシマ

No More Hiroshimas

Poems and translations

James Kirkup

SPOKESMAN

First published in 1983 in Japan by Kyoto Editions.
This edition published in 2004 by

Spokesman Books
Russell House, Bulwell Lane, Nottingham NG6 0BT
Phone 0115 9708318
Fax 0115 9420433
e-mail elfeuro@compuserve.com
www.spokesmanbooks.com

ISBN 0 85124 689 3

A CIP catalogue record is available from the British Library

Printed by the Russell Press Ltd. (phone 0115 9784505)

CONTENTS

ACKNOWLEDGEMENTS

'Hiroshima Revisited, 1982' was specially written for this collection of A-bomb poems.

'The Lantern-Floating Festival' first appeared in *Zen Contemplations* (Kyoto Editions).

'No More Hiroshimas' originally appeared in *The Times Literary Supplement,* and was first published in *Refusal to Conform* (Oxford University Press), then in *Japan Physical* (Kenkyusha, Tokyo).

'Ghosts, Fire, Water' originally appeared in *The Descent into the Cave* (Oxford University Press), and then in *Japan Physical* (Kenkyusha, Tokyo).

'White Shadows' originally appeared in *White Shadows, Black Shadows* (Dent) and then in *Japan Physical* (Kenkyusha, Tokyo).

'Bitter Peace' is part of the poem sequence 'Japan Marine', awarded first prize in the Japan P.E.N. Club's International Literary Competition. First printed in 'Prize-winning Entries, Japan P.E.N. Club Olympic Literary Prize', published in Tokyo by the Japan P.E.N. Club. Then in *Paper Windows: Poems from Japan* (Dent) and *Japan Physical* (Kenkyusha).

'Our New Baby' originally appeared in a slightly different form in *White Shadows, Black Shadows* (Dent).

'Not Cricket' was first printed in *Peace News,* then in *Paper Windows: Poems from Japan* (Dent) and in *Japan Physical* (Kenkyusha).

'Cena' first appeared in *Time and Tide*, then in *New Poems 1965*, in *Paper Windows: Poems from Japan* and in *Japan Physical*.

'Friends of the Neutron Bomb' first appeared in *Poets for Peace* issued by Hampstead CND, 1981.

The translations of Atomic Bomb poems by Toge Sankichi appeared in *Poetry Australia* and in my anthology of translations, *Modern Japanese Poetry*, edited and introduced by Professor A. R. Davis (University of Queensland Press). Ikeda Some's 'Umeboshi' is from the same collection.

'The Carol of the Four Wise Men', 'Nuclear News of the World', 'Neutron Memory', 'All Animals are Equal', 'B-29 Mission' and 'In Madrid – March 11' appear here for the first time.

Also by James Kirkup from Kyoto Editions:
Enlightenment (poetry poster / wall hanging)
The Forgetful Angels (Paul Klee poetry poster)
Zen Contemplations
Cold Mountain Poems: Interpretations from the Chinese
Dengonban Messages: one-line *haiku* and *senryu*
Scenes from Sutcliffe (portfolio of photographs/poems)
Ecce Homo: My Pasolini (poems and translations)
Poems Grim and Gay (in preparation)

PREFACE

My A-Bomb Biography

These poems all have their roots in one late afternoon at the 'War Ag' land workers' hostel outside Ponteland, Northumberland. The gang of workers had just returned from another sweltering day of 'labour on the land'– draining and ditching. As we entered the hostel we got the news that the first American Atom Bomb had been dropped on Japan, on the city of Hiroshima. It was the first time we had heard of that place that was to become a universal symbol of man's inhumanity towards his fellow-men.

We had become accustomed to air raids and 'buzz-bombs' and to our own casualty lists at home and abroad. But this new weapon left us nonplussed and incredulous. The date was August 6th, 1945. Its world-wide significance was at that time beyond our comprehension, and we did not realise that the date was to become an international anniversary for peace.

Three days later, on August 9th, we received the news of an even larger and more powerful plutonium bomb that had been dropped on the city of Nagasaki and had almost completely devastated it. The name was known to me only as the home of Madame Butterfly. But we began to realise the enormity of these acts of war that had annihilated hundreds of thousands of civilians.

At that time, all I knew about Japan was from my wartime readings of Arthur Waley's translation of *The Tale of Genji*. When peace was declared, I was liberated and started reading English or French or German translations of Japanese literature, ancient and modern. I also studied the history of Japanese art.

It was this passion for oriental painting that led me to visit, in London, the first exhibition of paintings devoted to the themes of atomic bomb horrors. They were by Iri Maruki and Toshiko Akamatsu, and were shown in Europe for the first time in 1955. These vividly realistic paintings made such a profound impression upon me that I went straight back to my room and wrote in longhand, at a single draft, the poem, 'Ghosts, Fire, Water' which I took straight back to the gallery, and laid it in the book of visitors' comments. Then I returned home and typed it out without any alterations and sent it to Kingsley Martin at *The New Statesman*, which had already published some of my work. It was rejected, without comment.

By that time, I had received a response from the woman who had organised the exhibition, expressing her admiration and gratitude, and urging me to send it to British newspapers and periodicals. I sent out many copies but they were all either ignored or politely rejected. However, I managed to include it in my next volume of poems, *The Descent into the Cave* (Oxford University Press), two years later, in 1957. There were no reviews mentioning the poem.

In 1959, I took up my first post in Japan, teaching English literature in Tohoku University in Sendai. As I later described in my volume of autobiography, *I, of All People* (Weidenfeld and Nicolson, 1988), the British Council did everything they could to prevent my appointment and departure, after interrogating me in their London offices.

In Japan, I visited Hiroshima and Nagasaki as soon as possible, and wrote my impressions of Hiroshima in 1960, 'No More Hiroshimas', which appeared in my new collection, *Refusal to Conform* (OUP, 1963). On various other visits to those cities I wrote 'The Lantern-Floating Festival', 'White Shadows', 'Hiroshima Revisited (1982)', 'Friends of the Neutron Bomb', 'The Carol of the Four Wise Men', 'Our New Baby' and various other poems that were widely published and commented on in Japan – but not in Britain.

I collected my A-Bomb poems in a volume entitled *No More Hiroshimas* in 1983 and sent it to all the British publishers who still published poetry. It was rejected by all of them. So I decided to publish it myself, at my own expense, and as I was then in the early 1980s teaching in Kyoto, I called my press 'Kyoto Editions'. I had discovered, in the enormous Kinokuniya bookstore in Osaka's

Umeda Station, a department that renewed and bound student theses, pamphlets and poetry collections. I designed the cover, with my name translated into Japanese by Makoto Tamaki.

When the book was ready, I sent out copies to all the British press, where it was ignored. No magazine mentioned it. So I just kept sending out copies to friends and to anyone I thought might be interested in it, until the first printing was exhausted. I had it reprinted by the bookshop, and by 1984 it had gone through four editions. I stamped the Peace Symbol in red on each cover.

Twenty years later, I was inspired to send a copy to Professor Ken Coates at the Bertrand Russell Peace Foundation. He at once offered to print it as a real book. So here it is, at long last.

James Kirkup
Andorra, April 2004

We are honoured to be able to publish James Kirkup's book of poems, and so to make reparation for the neglect which he has unjustly suffered in the British press. Our readers may judge whether it is possible that this neglect reflects a deeper Western guilt about events in Hiroshima, rather than a considered judgement on James Kirkup's poems.

Ken Coates
Bertrand Russell Peace Foundation

UMEBOSHI

An old woman of ninety remembers the explosion of the
A-bomb at Hiroshima

Well, that time ... let me see,
I fell over with the cupboard in the living-room.

The house shook and shook and shook and
I crawled out onto the roof.
I did not crawl of my own accord, naturally
I should rather say 'I was made to do it
By God or Buddha.'

O, what misery.
O, what pain.
I wanted the breath to be taken from my body
And to go to heaven.

It was on the third morning after the explosion
Someone put an *umeboshi* in my mouth.

'This old woman is dead,' they said. 'What a shame!'
They prayed the Buddhist prayer: '*Namu-amida, namu-amida.*'

'I am alive. I am alive,' I told them.
They put a big *umeboshi* in my mouth.

Umeboshi's nice and tasty, you know, so
I must express my thanks to the *umeboshi*, because
I soon got well again.

umeboshi: a pickled Japanese plum, a cheap and common delicacy.

(Translated from the Japanese of Ikeda Some by
James Kirkup and Michio Nakano.)

[13]

NO MORE HIROSHIMAS

At the station exit, my bundle in hand,
Early the winter afternoon's wet snow
Falls thinly round me, out of a crudded sun.
I had forgotten to remember where I was.
Looking about, I see it might be anywhere –
A station, a town like any other in Japan,
Ramshackle, muddy, noisy, drab; a cheerfully
Shallow impermanence: peeling concrete, litter, 'Atomic
Lotion, for hair fall-out,' a flimsy department store;
Racks and towers of neon, flashy over tiled and tilted waves
Of little roofs, shacks cascading lemons and persimmons,
Oranges and dark-red apples, shanties awash with rainbows
Of squid and octopus, shellfish, slabs of tuna, oysters, ice,
Ablaze with fans of soiled nude-picture books
Thumbed abstractedly by schoolboys, with second-hand looks.

The river remains unchanged, sad, refusing rehabilitation.
In this long, wide, empty official boulevard
The new trees are still small, the office blocks
Basely functional. The bridge a slick abstraction.
But the river remains unchanged, sad, refusing rehabilitation.

In the city centre, far from the station's lively squalor,
A kind of life goes on, in cinemas and hi-fi coffee bars,
In the shuffling racket of pin-table palaces and parlours,
The souvenir shops piled high with junk, kimonoed kewpie dolls,
Models of the bombed Industry Promotion Hall, memorial ruin
Tricked out with glitter-frost and artificial pearls.

Set in an awful emptiness, the modern tourist hotel is trimmed
With jaded Christmas frippery, flatulent balloons; in the hall,
A giant dingy iced cake in the shape of a Cinderella coach.

The contemporary stairs are treacherous, the corridors
Deserted, my room an overheated morgue, the bar in darkness.
Punctually, the electric chimes ring out across the tidy waste
Their doleful public hymn – the tune unrecognizable, evangelist.

Here atomic peace is geared to meet the tourist trade.
Let it remain like this, for all the world to see,
Without nobility or loveliness, and dogged with shame
That is beyond all hope of indignation. Anger, too, is dead.
And why should memorials of what was far
From pleasant have the grace that helps us to forget?

In the dying afternoon, I wander dying round the Park of Peace.
It is right, this squat, dead place, with its left-over air
Of an abandoned International Trade and Tourist Fair.
The stunted trees are wrapped in straw against the cold.
The gardeners are old, old women in blue bloomers, white aprons,
Survivors weeding the dead brown lawns around the Children's
    Monument.

A hideous pile, the Atomic Bomb Explosion Centre, freezing cold,
'Includes the Peace Tower, a museum containing
Atomic-melted slates and bricks, photos showing
What the Atomic Desert looked like, and other
Relics of the catastrophe.'

The other relics:
The ones that made me weep;
The bits of burnt clothing,
The stopped watches, the torn shirts,
The twisted buttons,
The stained and tattered vests and drawers,

The ripped kimonos and charred boots,
The white blouse polka-dotted with atomic rain, indelible,
The cotton summer pants the blasted boys crawled home in, to
    bleed
And slowly die.

Remember only these.
They are the memorials we need.

Hiroshima, New Year, 1960

GHOSTS, FIRE, WATER

On the Hiroshima panels by Iri Maruki and Toshiko Akamatsu

These are the ghosts of the unwilling dead,
Grey ghosts of that imprinted flash of memory
Whose flaming and eternal instant haunts
The speechless dark with dread and anger.

Grey, out of pale nothingness their agony appears.
Like ash they are blown and blasted on the wind's
Vermilion breathlessness, like shapeless smoke
Their shapes are torn across the paper sky.

These scarred and ashen ghosts are quick
With pain's unutterable speech, their flame-cracked flesh
Writhes and is heavy as the worms, the bitter dirt;
Lonely as in death they bleed, naked as in birth.

They greet each other in a ghastly paradise,
These ghosts who cannot come with gifts and flowers.
Here they receive each other with disaster's common love,
Covering one another's pain with shrivelled hands.

They are not beautiful, yet beauty is in their truth.
There is no easy music in their silent screams,
No ordered dancing in their grief's distracted limbs.
Their shame is ours. We, too, are haunted by their fate.

In the shock of flame, their tears brand our flesh,
We twist in their furnace, and our scorching throats
Parch for the waters where the cool dead float.
We press our lips upon the river where they drink, and drown.

Their voices call to us, in pain and indignation:
'This is what you have done to us!'
Their accusation is our final hope. Be comforted.
Yes, we have heard you, ghosts of our indifference,

We hear your cry, we understand your warnings.
We, too, shall refuse to accept our fate!
Haunt us with the truth of our betrayal
Until the earth's united voices shout refusal, sing your peace!

Forgive us, that we had to see your passion to remember
What we must never again deny: *Love one another.*

London, 1955

THE LANTERN-FLOATING FESTIVAL

The paper lanterns are sold by old women, little children
at stalls among the willows along the crowded river bank.

Long oblongs of paper – red, green, yellow, dusted with gold,
hastily inscribed with brush and watery Chinese ink –
crammed with the characters of names, prayers, poems, messages.

The papers are fastened round upright struts like cheap
    chopsticks
that are fixed at the ends of a cross of laths, the lantern's floats.
At the heart of the cross, a small candle stuck on a nail.

The mourners write their poems, light their candles. The
    lanterns'
colours, ambered by the little flame, delicate and pure.

They are borne carefully, the lanterns for the dead, in both hands,
As if the bearers were holding a precious fluid, a fragile treasure,
or the very soul of someone loved, someone still loved –
borne before them in praying hands, with the respect
that is the only proof of memory, of former life.

Those who are remembering the dead
stand in long lines on the dark shore
and crowd together on the steep steps of unlighted stone, souls
waiting for waftage on the altar and embankment of the grieving
    river.

The small flames beat like moths, like hearts,
or heave like sighs, like human breath in last release
within the paper shells frail as their bearers.

At the river's quiet verge, whose dark water laps
the steps leading down into its darkening sky,
the summer mourners crouch in blue and white cotton clothes,
    simple,
thin feet on worn wooden pattens.

One careless virgin flusters her flame, and
the entire lantern flares in an instant,
singeing the sleeves of neighbours.
Her loved one's name,
hastily written in gathering darkness
with a wretched brush and weak ink
is obliterated, as he was, by a flash of fire.
Some have inscribed the name of a cat,
a pet rabbit, a tame rat,
a dog who did not come home,
a canary, a grasshopper, a cicada,
a child's summer insect in a bamboo cage, now ash.

All crouch, do not kneel,
but with murmured prayers to Buddha
and sometimes
the chime of a tiny portable gong
gently launch their lighted craft,
wafting them softly away from the bank
with cheap scented paper fans
or hands rippling the water
in beckoning gestures of farewell,
in farewell gestures, beckoning
the dead to the living, that they may return,
if only in a dream,
and speak their peace.

The air fogged with incense
and the surges of dumb temple gongs
shroud us all, shroud
the lanterns that cling to the banks, refuse
to leave the life they could not hate
for what perhaps may be an even deeper misery.

The lanterns cluster stubbornly like set jewels, or
a stiff arrangement of flowers
reflected in the gleaming ripples,
and will not budge.

No breath of wind, no current takes them.
Their unwillingness to go is human, their persistence spectral.
Only two – who are they, who were they? –
for some reason leave the banks and float, lighted still,
downstream, to negotiate the arches of a bridge – but then
founder, flicker, flutter, extinguished on a sudden bend ...

Now whole fleets of lanterns
like battling argosies
lock together, and one,
bursting into flame,
ignites a chain of paper sails –
meaningless reaction, meaningless cause and
meaningless effect: just so does nuclear death
rob death of its one distinction –
a meaning.

No one weeps
and no one smiles.
All are part of Buddha nature,
the Buddha
that neither smiles nor weeps.

But in this festival of ghosts,
who are the apparitions, who
the living?

These survivors,
freaks of destiny,
are they still human?
Do they burn with a flame
of healthy blood?

Or are they also spectres,
floating lighted lanterns
in memory of themselves?

– I pass among them,
a stranger,
outsider,
unnoticed as a ghost.

Hiroshima, August 1966

HIROSHIMA REVISITED 1982

Now all round the shiny, reconstructed railway station
still the messy hodge-podge of planless architecture –
vulgar, brash, lively as the giant Toshiba neon sign flashing
(with questionable sincerity) its mechanical 'Welcome to
   Hiroshima'.

Somewhere beyond all this materialistic illusion of life
there are tranquil temple gardens, shrines, stones, lanterns,
Buddhas, ancient sculptures in weathered cryptomeria wood,
calligraphies, chantings, gongs, prayers, veils of incense.

But this is here and now, this very morning, in miracle Japan
that is one enormous neon signboard adrift in the Pacific.
Strictly speaking, no advertising allowed in the Park of Peace,
but everywhere the slick modern ashtrays bear the slogan, fake-
   virile,
'Smokin' Clean' – Japanese ad man's American ad man's lie.
The shaved-ice merchants pour their harsh false chemical dyes
in approaches lined with souvenir stalls of memorial frippery.

So let us, in clouds of pigeons, enter the Park of Peace –
Some granite blocks 'from the youth of Fort William in Scotland'
are dutifully inscribed with customary messages, still dreams, still
moving, of international brotherhood, harmony and universal peace.
A rhymed jingle by Edmund Blunden shames the stone it wasted.

But here is something finer, the massive root of a camphor tree
from the fire-stormed Kokutaiji Temple Grounds, beside which
the usual banal modern abstract sculpture of an abstraction,
'The Spiritual World,' by Matetsu Takemoto, is pretentious and
   superfluous.

– Baby-blue plastic seats degrade the ruined Industry Promotion
    Hall.

For this place is the trivialization of earth's greatest tragedy:
the 'Cenorial' is an American Frontier covered wagon, abstracted,
whose weak arch frames a baseball stadium's grim banks of
    floodlights.
Old ladies are still sweeping up piles of trash, Coke and beer cans,
    dog-ends and lunchboxes.

Hideous, the Seiko clock tower, the cheap kitsch statuary
in socialist-realist city-centre style, the sugary sentimentality of
the Children's Monument, its useless hanks of folded paper cranes,
the Belfry a prosaic concrete dome on four cracked concrete pillars –
only the bronze bell authentic: it strikes to the marrow of my bones.

And on a notice-board beside it, someone prophetically
has crossed out that one word – 'Peace'.

Four Atomic Bomb Poems by Toge Sankichi

★

AT A FIRST AID POST

You
Who have no channels for tears when you weep
No lips through which words can issue when you howl
No skin for your fingers to grip with when you writhe in torment

You

Your squirming limbs all smeared with blood and slimy sweat
 and lymph
Between your closed lids the glaring eyeballs show only a thread
 of white
On your pale swollen bellies only the perished elastic that held
 up your drawers
You who can no longer feel shame at exposing your sheltered sex
O who could believe that
Only minutes ago
You were all schoolgirls fresh and appealing

In the scorched and raw Hiroshima
Out of dark shuddering flames
You no longer the human creatures you had been
Scrambled and crawled one after the other
Dragged yourselves along as far as this open ground
To bury in the dusts of agony
Your frizzled hair on skulls almost as bald as heads of Buddhist
 saints

Why should you have to suffer like this
Why suffer like this
What is the reason

What reason
And you
Do not know
How you look nor
What your humanity has been turned into

You are remembering
Simply remembering
Those who until this morning were
Your fathers mothers brothers sisters
(Would any of them recognize you now if they met you)
Remembering your homes where you used to sleep wake eat
(In a single flash all the flowers on their hedges were blasted
And no one knows where their ashes lie)
Remembering remembering
Here with your fellow-creatures who one by one gradually moving
Remembering
Those days when
You were daughters
Daughters of humankind

TO MISS ...

You live on deep in the ditch of an alley in the slums
At the bomb-blasted site of the Transport Corps
The stony road haunted by a vision of horses
Kicking the air above their torn bellies.

Only a year ago, rainy days would allow you to go out
To the hospital, because you could hide then behind your
    umbrella.
But now that you never come out to expose to our view
The memory of that flash the shadow of the B 29
That thundered down upon your face your eyes your nose

One arm ripped away by an avalanching house
The other remaining for you to make a living by ...
What sad stitches you keep knitting day by day
When bitter blood stains your fingers
In this quiet corner of the town
Humming softly with windmills
The voices of children playing in vegetable plots.

Never have I dared to call on you.
But today I am coming to see you
Along this ruined path.

Welts like serpents
Your skin's sickly lustre baldly naked
Bring back to me my native feelings of compassion for you
As you sit there before me caked with oozing pus
In this hole of constant pain
The heart once of a tender girl now shrivelled to a stone
In the rosy light of the setting sun.

O let me tell you now my dear
Of this burning wish we have that wells up from our souls
Of this passion fierce enough to melt the coldest heart
Of the desperate battle in which thousands of your pictures
Shall overcome the powers of darkness in this world
(Under the droning shadows that even now
Keep looming over us again)

Of that hard-won moment when
Our indignation
And your curse
Shall open into radiance of loveliest flowers!

THE NIGHT

Eyes aching
Brimming
In the swarming lights of Hiroshima
Everywhere the swollen scars
On shiny keloid skin
Wet streaks writhing
Muddy mazes stinking of decay
Blasted trunks dotted with flabby buds
And sunk in the drizzling rain
Women's eyes redder than the fires of their cigarettes
Their branded thighs laid open to the view.

O Hiroshima
Sterile erection shattered by an atomic bomb
Women are barren
Men shoot listless sperm
While in that resplendent area of leasehold land
The bowers of Hijiyama Park
The tail-light of a gliding limousine is being born
From the arc lamps of the A-Bomb Casualty Survey Centre
In the air of night
That throbs with New Mexican jazz.

(In window-frames across the river
Feral women are languorously stretching
Removing their petals
Discarding their pistils
As they make ready for nightwork.)

On the roof of the station cradling blinded trains
Mindless characters are spilling from the electric newsflash
Telling of second, third, hundredth A-bomb tests

To the bleeding apparition of a drunkard
Shambling away out of nowhere
The lank shadow of a soldier rising
In a boat scraping the rocks of the black river
When the tide of evening floods the banks
Effacing the footprints left by scrap-metal pickers.

Listen
Dark-blue flutterings disturb the heavens
Across the night towards the dawn
Or from the dawn towards the night
Over Hiroshima's leprous map of lights
Some hanging in the distance
Some suspended half-way
Some trying fearfully to forget
Some desperately seething
Some trembling
Some dying
Crawling on their own blood
Retreading from the doomed memory
The sad nebulae of Hiroshima
Mute and sunken in

The darknesses of history.

THE VISION

Always we have this burning vision:

A city on the delta of some volcanic island, where
The windows of buildings are blazing with colourless flames of
    fire
Traffic signals trapping fire-robed refugees and then
Releasing them again
The big station clock obliterated buried in fires from chimneys
Fire-cargoed ships sailing in and sailing out from the piers
And with sudden soundless hoots of fire
Desperate expresses dragging forth phimoses of fire
Women nestling the fire of pus in their crotches
And when a foreigner walks by striking his lighter
Many beggars in black scuttle after him for alms of fire
Behold that man scavenging a fire-tipped cigarette over there.

Always we live with this flaring vision of a fire that
Never dies
Never is extinguished.
And is there any one of us who could deny
That all of us are already on fire?

At night above the floods of radiant lights
The sheet upon sheet of dazzling neon
I sense a sea of flames heaving up into
The dark tunnels of the midnight skies
Thronged with our disfigured brothers
Feet upon feet hands upon hands
All blood and licked by the cruel tongues of fire
Splintered brains
Galaxies burning at the stake
Collapsing

[31]

In roses of fire in blue bowers of sparks
Whirling gales of firestorms
Out of darkness screaming
Indignation regret resentment grief
Curses hatred pleadings wailings
Until all these moaning voices stream from the earth into the sky.

No longer are we what we used to be, ourselves, but other beings
With our own bodies still, but with a burning stink,
With peeled skins bald heads we go
Branded with all the marks of the Atomic Tribe
Humans bereft of the right to live as humans.
Now even a test on some lagoon in the farthest reaches of the
     oceans
Makes us jump
For we know each bomb is hanging on its parachute of blackness
Over our melting-pot.

Watch the way the tongueless flames are dancing
The lungless tongues are writhing
Teeth piercing lips
Lips spouting liquid fire
And how these voiceless fires stream through all the earth to
     bring
A blazing Hiroshima to London
A blasting Hiroshima to New York
An incandescent Hiroshima to Moscow

Watch how the voiceless fires go dancing round the world
With gestures of pain and indignation.
Yes, we are all fires blazing with the vision that we fuel
Like forests of furnace fire
Like seas of liquid fire
Lapping the earth in flame and fever.

Yes, we are nothing but a mad mass of fire
Blazing passionately against the next scheme
Of the devils of nuclear holocaust.

*(I am grateful to Professor Fumiko Miura and to Miss Akiko Takemoto for their help and advice in translating these poems by Toge Sankichi. ** James Kirkup.)*

WHITE SHADOWS

On a photograph of the white shadow left by a
man annihilated in the atomic bombing of Hiroshima

It was another morning, another morning.
A morning like any other, of dust and death.
A morning of war: raids, speeches, warnings.
In wartime, all mornings are alike.

Your were crossing a bridge in Hiroshima,
A bridge of plain cement, a place without mystery.
Below, the grey river ran as always, going somewhere,
Metalled and moved by the early summer sun.

The sun, that cast your shadow clearly, a healthy black.
It was the shadow of a complete man, someone
With a life, a personality, a past: but
Moving through a present that could have no future.

What were you thinking? Were you feared, hated, loved?
Were you late for work? Sad or sick? Artist, student?
Photographer or newsman returning home after a night out?
What was your plan for the day? Who were you, shadow?

I do not know your name, your age, your blood type.
And now I shall never see your face, hear your voice.
No one will ever know your name, your age, your blood type.
And are there any left who remember your face, your voice?

Now, the name, the face, the voice no longer matter.
A 'plane drilled the blue, as they often did. The river ran.
Your shadow was black: then white – the flash was all
And nothing. You were not there to hear the rest.

[34]

Your shade – poor, forked human creature – fled
Like a mist of dew on morning glories. Your breath
Evaporated, taken away, lost soul, before
You even had time to scream. Your shade was white.

★

That white
Is blacker than black,
That shadow
Is more than a shade.

That shape
Is whiter than white.
That whiteness
Is blacker than night.

Blacker than black,
Blacker than white.
Blacker than blast and blight,
Blacker than light.

Whiter than black,
Whiter than sight,
Black as the flash,
Blacker than fright.

White as the bomb,
White as a scar,
Black as the womb,
Black as war.

Blacker than breath,
Blacker than cold.
Whiter than death,
Whiter than gold.

That white
Is blacker than black,
That shadow
Is more than a shade.

★

You vanished, and a whole world, a fragrance, a name
Vanished with you. A Shade. It was death indeed,
Death in absence. – But you left behind you, in the black rain
Of poisoned ash, your own memorial, your own white shadow.

It stretched companionless across the road, until
Its head (hatless) was lost over the edge of the bridge.
Yours was the long shadow of early morning, another morning,
Another morning in early summer, when shadows are blackest.

The white shadow shows no feet. You were already a ghost.
(In Japan, they say, ghosts have no feet.) – No arms.
Only the elementary fork, the primitive crotch,
And the torso, naked, alone, archaic. No hero's.

★

Who owns him? Was he your father? Your brother?
Your lover, was he? Or your enemy, friend, classmate?
Was this white memory once your husband of flesh and blood?
All I know is, he was a man, a human being like myself.

Questions are hard, but it is worse to remain silent.
Nor can we afford not to look. We must see all, and say all
To satisfy the dead who died with such indignity, the shades
That are watching us, white and speechless. We cannot look away.

*

You whose shadow once was black as soot,
Black the vivid black of all living shadows –
You whose shadow moved beside you everywhere
Like a favourite hound at heel, mysterious, silent.

You exchanged your shadow and your shape,
O Peter Schlemihl, for one no longer black,
For the white shadow that is waiting here, a livid
Black, in all of us today, in all of us today.

We too have sold our shadows to the devil.
We have gained the whole world
But lost the fragrance of our immortal souls.
A race without shadows, we too are doomed.

Led by the ignorant and the mad, we live in worlds
Where black is white, and white is black,
Where leaders say that peace can not be found
Except in continued bombings of the helpless.

Where war is peace, and peace is war,
Where bombs are good, and people bad.
Where sleep is wake and eat is starve.
Where live is die. Where love is kill.

[37]

*

We look upon this calm, white monument
And see in it an image of ourselves.
Today, our shadows walk beside us still,
But they are no longer black, no longer black.

We are all white shadows, anonymous as yours.
No longer human, we cross bridges,
   walk in our shadows' snow.
Grey rivers are metalled and moved by the sun. It is
Another morning. And all our mornings are alike.

Tokyo, December 6th 1967

YOUNG LOVERS' FIERY DEATH PROTEST AGAINST WAR

With all their clothes on –
Unusual for these two, so frank in passion and
Most eloquent when naked – they put their arms
Round one another, lay down among the derelicts
Of a used-car dump. Silently. Japan jumped all about them.
It was the neon midnight of New Year's Eve.

The temple bells, banged by severe monks,
Slowly massaged the icy air
With warm waves of vibrations,
A steady storm of breakers on Pacific shores.

One hundred and eight notes,
To the precise number of one year's sins:
How small a number for one man, how small!
They welled like giant teardrops, one
Upon the other, sounding a wilderness of nothing.
Stars creaked like hard snow underfoot.

The squashed cars cast shadows of traffic accidents,
A nightmare of horns forever silenced, brakes rusted,
Lights dipped once and for all, internal combustion
Finally busted, big ends gone, tyres flat
As rats ironed out on city expressways,
Windscreens riddled, galaxied, steering columns
Snapped. No rearview mirrors. Modern Japan.

He had placed beside them a can of gasoline
Whose tremulous tin occasionally clanged
Cold notes of an unearthly plangency, wailings
That mingled with the welling bells
Or sang like firecrackers, pistol shots.

In the can a pale green plastic siphon was
Already inserted, leaning like a flower in a vase,
Waiting for the master arranger's final touch.
As the bells tolled, the liquid rose, and pulsed
Like icy piss over their winter rags.

On that one hundred and eighth stroke, or just before,
She raised a hand blue with cold and neon,
And, with a gesture too benumbed to be like
Defiant snapping of her fingers, clicked and sparked
The cheap lighter in the form of a jewelled pistol.

Asakusa, New Year, 1967

DEATH OF A JAPANESE ESPERANTIST

In memory of Tadanoshin Yui

Outside Prime Minister Sato's official residence
you, Tandanoshin Yui, an old scholar
and a lifelong student of Esperanto,
kneeled down, but not in prayer.

It was a cold day, but clear. November.
You kept your old overcoat on,
though it was not to keep you warm.
There was a deeper flame.

Your old suit and overcoat
were drenched in icy gasoline.
Looking for the green star of hope,
you struck your last match.

You left behind you this pure
statement of your intentions:
'I am fully aware that it is useless for
a mere citizen like myself to appeal to the government...'

Such is democracy. Your act was pure,
but useless. The wars continue.
Okinawa now returned: yet still apart...
Japan protests with violence, not peace.

Your suicide was gentle in its peace,
its humble indignation. Let us remember
your peace, before we strike the final match
of mad mass-destruction by nuclear neutron bombs!

You, at least, old man,
were sane. We cannot say as much of ourselves,
or of our world, our self-appointed leaders,
most dangerous in their sheer stupidity.

My verdict on you, old scholar:
death of sound mind.

Nagoya, 1970. Revised 1982.

IN MEMORIAM: BERTRAND RUSSELL

In another February, on a Sunday afternoon eight years ago,
I wept for you, and for a world that could reject your voice.

You were so frail, so ancient; yet stronger than us all.
You stood beside me on a platform in Trafalgar Square
among the toothless lions of a tyrannous imperial pride,
under the shadow of Nelson strutting in the falling snow.

Your head was bare, and your wild white hair
blazed like your mind in the wind of whirling flakes.
Your face, the mask of a tragic hawk,
was sad and bitter as you cried your warnings and defiance
at the armed forces of error, the police of Britain,
the criminal politicians, the priests of power, the insane
manufacturers of arms and poison gas and atom bombs,
inhuman profiteers all, sucking the blood of human misery.

You stood alone before the gathered heads of microphones,
tilted intelligently, raised like vipers, cobras about to strike.
– But like a saint, or like Apollo, god of poetry and music,
you charmed them into peace. You won their love with love,
with the fearless beauty of your mind, your noble voice.

Dear man, I remember your friendship for the lost and helpless,
and the grasp of your withered hand in mine that February day,
delicate but strong. I remember the wise humour of your smile,
twisted yet pure; the sparkle in your hooded, sombre eyes;
the deep lines in your cheeks; the nose like a mountain peak.
– And O, that great and simple brow – so vast, so calm, so full!

Most of all, I remember how you taught me to have courage
to defy the world in solitude; how to disarm
the dangerous stupidity of man, using weapons not of this world –
intellect with love; wit with pity; candour with compassion.

Now, in a foreign snow, my tears are falling for you,
and for the world, that did not heed your warning cries.

Tokyo, February 3rd 1970

BLACK SHADOWS

In memory of Martin Luther King

I can hear from New Orleans
Funeral jazz.

Memphis, Nashville, Atlanta
Blow horns of grief.

All the jazzbands of the South
Trumpet your murder.

What has our world become? Are we all mad?
Good man, forgive us.

★

When I look at your calm face, I see
The courage of your death.

It is our shame
That such courage was necessary.

You knew that bullet from a white rifle
Would one day seek your flesh.

You walked in danger every day
With sad humility.

Not wishing to be chosen thus by fate,
Yet knowing you must drink that cup.

Your wife and children weep now
For a man who was more than a father.

You were a father to all of us.
We did not know it till you were gone.

Now we understand your gentleness
Too late. Why must we hate?

Why must we kill our brothers?
Why suffer this shame of wars upon wars?

*

You who told us war and violence are bad
Died of war and violence.

You were a man of peace and mercy,
But received neither.

May your spirit help us
To become your disciples.

Let us raise no monument to you
But human peace and mercy.

Let us stand, as you did,
Against a world of murder and deceit.

What has our world become? Are we all mad?
Good man, forgive us.

FROGS IN THAILAND COMMIT MASS SUICIDE
(Newspaper report)
to Kusano Shinpei,
Master of the Frogs

How wise they are!
Knowing the end is near
They exterminate themselves, rather than
Face the ignominy of atomic death,
Of neutron negation.

These frogs once lived a happy life.
They ate, drank, bred and croaked in freedom,
They hadn't a care in the world.
They were always great jumpers.
How they could jump!
That is why they had such long,
Noble, meaty thighs.
O, how they loved to jump!

But in their blissful existence
Came a cloud, a sadness, a sick fear
Of an uncertain but terrible future.

They were helpless.
There was nothing they could do
To save themselves, except
To jump, and jump and jump –
For jumping was their whole existence.

They jumped to horrible effect:
They used their springs of flesh
To hurl themselves upon the piercing
Foot-long spines of one thorny bush.

[47]

Such a bush in the tropics
Has thousands of fierce spikes.
But they were not enough to accommodate
The frogs' mad rush of mysterious despair.

So they played a macabre leapfrog,
Thrusting themselves upon each other,
Death-coitus orgy on spits of thorn,
Catapulted copulation until
There were scores of frogs,
Pitiful Saint Sebastians, arrow-pierced,
On every long spine's lancing dirk.

It was a poignant *auto-da-fé*.
As if on long darts or vicious needles
They were impaled through the heart,
Skewered for some atomic barbecue.

Like rats abandoning a sinking ship,
Or lemmings drowning in Norwegian fjords.
– Had the impending visit of the God of War,
President Lyndon B. Johnson of the US of A,
Put the fear of hell into the innocents
Till they were scared shitless?
– For it was another Massacre of the Innocents,
Another Saint Bartholomew's Eve!

★

Only the week before,
So the informed sources say,
Frogs and toads by their tens of thousands
Fought losing battles with each other,
Great armies of frogs and toads

[48]

Fighting insensately, killing each other off
In a war to end all frog wars,
To put a final stop to population explosion.
No one was spared
In these losing battles with despair,
Battles fought to the death
To defend only the right to die.

What could they see
That we poor mortals fail to see?
What have they heard? Some whisper of fright,
Some ghastly rumour we shut our ears to?
What have they tasted on the air –
A tang of radioactive dust?
Have they seen white shadows,
Livid blacknesses,
Shades of hellish ash,
Ghosts of atomic rain?

Why cannot we see what they have seen,
And stop before it is too late?
Are we as helpless as predestined frogs?
Why cannot we hear what they have heard?
Is it a sound beyond human hearing,
That only frogs can catch?
Why cannot we taste
The contaminated air of hydrogen bomb holocausts?

Are we, too, about to be impaled
On millions of megatons
And self-massacred by atomic warheads
Of sharp Intercontinental Ballistic Missiles?
Are we, too,

[49]

With all our wealth of science, war and want,
Helpless as gentle frogs and peaceable toads?

★

May our leaders take a lesson from
This augury and omen, these Thailand Ides of March
That came at Christmas upon the earth to save us – and learn
From these creatures' brave example.
There have been stern critics
Of the moral rectitude of such mass assassinations,
Who say such things are permissible
Only when hydrogen or neutron bombs are dropped.

But I say it was not suicide.
They were right to prefer death to
Deadly life or living hell,
To be true ghosts,
Not white shadows in blackened sepulchres,
Not corpses in the White House of the mind.
Better to kill oneself than to exist
Pitifully in fear and misery and pain incurable,
Than to be slaughtered *en masse*,
Inhumanly, insanely, by
A manicured finger on a plastic button.

★

We are all frogs and toads.
We mean no harm to anyone, but we are all
Impaled, transfixed already
Upon the thorns of death, the pale
Spires of unbelief. Like Shelley,
We fall upon the thorns of life, we bleed ...

Bleed to disgusting death upon the thorns
That we alone have cultivated and commanded
In this former garden of our pleasant earth.

Boxing Day, 1967

BITTER PEACE

Now the pale sands' long, light autumn emptiness
Lies bright with narrow pools of sun and sea –
Blue backwaters in the low, mysterious dunes,
Or shallow ocean-parallels, calm troughs of brine
In waves of sand, profound aquaria in stranded rocks.

In the brief sun-sleep of the warm half-morning
Bleach the drawn-up boats, with pointed prow
And curves of white on faded blue; worn rowlocks,
Rope-lashed oars. The rusty baling-can
Beneath the bare plank seats is tilted vacantly

With silence, broken shells, a finger-breadth of sand.
– And here, among the phantom nets and sails, the ghosts
Of summer fishermen and shouting boys, another ghost
In dark clothes wanders, wounded and remote, dwarfed
By the solitude, the ocean's leaning skies.

He wanders down the empty miles of sand and shore,
Pausing, stooping: here a broken fan, and here a shattered bowl.
He picks dead rags. The black ships are shoals of poisoned fish.
His ruined shadow trails among the relics, shells and blasted
    bones,
The scarred corpses of a crime that turned to ash a summer day.

His eyes are fixed upon the ground that moves from step to step.
His bleeding hands, as in a long dream, ache to seize
Some wonder, some last glittering remembrancer, some sign,
Token of love or life or human happiness, some gleam
Of trust – but only dead words scrawled on shreds of dirty paper.

No message, talisman, no scrap of golden wreckage, garland
Cast away by sailors careless on a peaceful southern sea.
No. There is nothing in the wilderness that war has made:
Only a child's lost kite, one yen, a chopstick in the sand.
– A flagon of rice-wine, dry, contains this survivor's poem.

Minamata and Nagasaki

OUR NEW BABY

A Neutron Nativity for Now
(*to the tune of 'Away in a Manger'*)

Away in brown paper
a monster is born:
his bones black with strontium
his bowels all torn.

A test in the unclean sky
showered dust where he lay –
no nuclear deterrent
keeps leukaemia at bay.

His heart is inhuman
his sex is obscure –
the ox and the ass
are six-headed for sure.

The little boy Jesus
no crying he makes –
but the ox and the ass
frighten him when he wakes.

A star in the bright sky
made his gold halo melt,
radiated the shepherds
and the kings as they knelt.

His bald head inflated
with fallout so free –
he's as radioactive
as an H-babe can be.

[54]

His mother's womb withered
and she burst with his birth,
who was born blind to save us
from this hell here on earth.

Kyoto, May 1ˢᵗ 1982

THE CAROL OF THE FOUR WISE MEN

We four kings of Orient are –
Gaspard, Melchior and Balthazar.
And our fourth is Hiroshima.

We bring the God-child gifts
of gold, frankincense and myrrh.
– What do you bring, Hiroshima?

       I bring the memory of my disgrace, and man's.
       I bring my city's sufferings, and Nagasaki's.
       I bring my fiery blast, and poisoned rains.

Is that all, Hiroshima? Surely
such offerings are hardly suitable
for One who is the Prince of Peace?

       I bring this capsule of reinforced lead
       wherein are enshrined the indestructible
       sacred treasures of our nuclear wastes
       intended for peaceful purposes only…
       Even sunk to the deepest dungeons of the seas
       they shall continue mystically to irradiate
       the Holy Child with every nuclear disease,
       poisoning all creatures of the oceans, and all
       who live upon the gifts that come from them.
       The animals and shepherds, too, are scarred,
       as are the fishermen of Minamata and Bikini
       with death's degeneration: and even you,
       come from afar,
       who three kings of Orient are,
       shall not survive that blinding star.

You're really going much too far,
dear Hiroshima, bringing in Nagasaki too.
Can you not promise something
a little more pleasant for our Heavenly King?

I also bring this bomb of steel, this missile
full of electrons, neutrons, and divine protons
to honour the Christ-child with
one vast multi-megaton explosion
a million times more sunny than the sun at noon –
to fill his little crib with light
from God – but fiercer, more intolerable and
eternally and infinitely bright!

NUCLEAR NEWS OF THE WORLD

In this gritty file photo
of starving homeless refugees
we see the sorry end of man –
another banality of the daily press.

Huddled together, squatting
on withered haunches, as if to defecate
they turn to the TV camera's
inhuman intrusion upon their misery
the look, blank with indifference,
of someone pissing in public,
careless of opinion, beyond censure,
gazing indifferently over their shoulders
at the press photographers of the world,
the well-fed international newshawks
as if they were not there at all, as if
they themselves were doing something else,
or living out this nightmare in another place.

Soldiers in jungle jumpsuits
level at these helpless waifs
the very latest in submachineguns.
– But their prisoners no longer care.
They know nothing of the neutron bomb.
They are not even victims any more.

Crouched in the middle of
some dusty tropical track, and parched with thirst,
they cover their heads from the sun
with a skeletal arm, a bit of old rag.
They suffer silently, past complaining.
They do not even know they are suffering.

So they will not bother to look up
at the tiny missile of the future
that in a minute will drop on them
immeasurable megatons

or dart its radiation down their veins, and leave
the Presidential Palace standing.

NOT CRICKET

I hear continually on the lips of men
Who fought in wars, who slaved in prison camps
Of captors' cruelties, starvation, lingering death,
Of tortures, atrocities, inhuman rage.

We are all prisoners of one another,
And all our captors are ourselves.
We are all beasts. But beasts
Do not disgrace each other as do men.

I, too, remember brutal overseers
In the labour camps of Britain, men
Who could only relish power
If they could degrade, mock, punish

With violence as sad as any commandant's,
With anger that revealed the heart of war.
– I remember also those who sheltered me,
Although they had no cause, and suffered for it.

I remember those in foreign camps
Who allowed themselves to love their captors.
And were loved. On both sides
A common brotherhood survived, a Christmas truce.

Not for us to rant of war's bad taste,
To issue pleas for decency, fair play.
If we permit our governments to arm for peace,
We sanction war, and must expect unpleasantnesses.

Hiroshima

NEUTRON MEMORY

Will there be anyone to memorize my poems?
(As they once memorized the poems of those other
poètes maudits – Mandelstam, Akhmatova…)

As even today the faithful memorize,
in many lands, the poems of so many
unknown poets, those in prison or

in 'psychiatric wards,' in gulags, labour camps,
torture cells, re-education centres, penal colonies –
the concentrated poetry of real pain.

– I do not care if all my poems are forgotten
if theirs might live on in the memories of man.
But memory, the everlasting word

no longer lasts for ever: neutralized,
only the printed page may still survive,
unradiated, unrepentant, slightly scorched –

but with no one left to read it, or remember it.

FRIENDS OF THE NEUTRON BOMB

Well, it'll get rid of
the one or two people I love,
but it will not get rid of
all the people I loathe:
Mrs Margaret Thatcher
President Ronald Reagan
and so on and so on.

The best buildings
will be left standing, more
or less, but also
some of the most vile, along with:
Mrs Margaret Thatcher
President Ronald Reagan
and so on and so on.

What gets me is that
the very people who made it possible –
politicians, heads of state – will be
preserved in radiation-proof cells:
Mrs Margaret Thatcher
President Ronald Reagan
and so on and so on.

While those who had the sense
to oppose the obscenity will all be gone.
So what we have to do is plain and clear –
neutralize the Friends of the Neutron Bomb:
Mrs Margaret Thatcher
President Ronald Reagan
and so on and so on... (*ad infinitum...*)

ALL ANIMALS ARE EQUAL

Zoos are concentration camps for animals.
The lords of creation
are imprisoned in them
by men who perhaps mean well
but who are really no better than
grinning tormentors.

In every zoo I visit, I can sense
the heartbreak and the boredom
of the beasts who should be free.

And my own heart breaks, too,
when I watch the hyena
still, after many years of useless anguish,
trying to scratch his way out –
when I see the mad stare
on the faces of neurotic tigers,
the hopeless lethargy of lions,
the misery of monkeys,
the insane gabble of tropical birds
who cannot bring the sky inside their cages
and sing with grief
at their separation from the humble sparrows –
humble, but free.

They all preserve a natural animal dignity:
even in despair, dejection, loneliness and sorrow,
they show a nobility far above ours –
for we, too, who go to watch our dumb friends
are their tormentors, and we can laugh
in safety, being free (or so we think) ...
The mighty black gorilla

sits with his back to us – so rude! –
the seals refuse to play for us,
no foxes will beg, no ostriches be cute.
The panda chews insipid bamboos
and cannot be persuaded to have an adorable baby,
the sad dromedaries have a haughty look,
the polar bears beg for buns, ingratiatingly, but
with one massive paw ready to claw and swipe ...

The zoo officials excuse all this dementia
by claiming that zoos protect endangered species.
Well, the preservation of the gnu or the crested ibis
is not as important as the loss of one guinea-pig's liberty
and cannot be justified by
the slow extinction of a million other creatures
deprived of native jungle, savannah, forest, desert, veldt,
and whose damned souls languish day and night
in the animal concentration camps
of Tokyo, New York, Peking, Berlin, Vincennes, Regent's Park –
Auschwitz, Dachau, Buchenwald, Treblinka, Mathausen,
    Theresienstadt.

THE ASS

Sweet innocent,
long-eared as fate,
stubbly spine and
scruffy mane,
tail like old rope;
roughly bearded,
a clown's quiet eyes
and homely stance.

Yet you are the cleanest
and toughest of them all.
Your strength is in that sweetness.
You carried Jesus.
– Is that a gallows in the background,
a signpost,
or a cross?

CENA

A crowded Last
Supper, thirteen heads,
Twenty-six hands, some
Under the table's
Long linenfold skirts,
Elbows getting in the way,
Feet in sandals kicked
Under the stout trestles,
Fingers dipped in dishes,
Breaking bread, carafe
Decanting acid wine,
Dark, muddy, poor stuff,
John, James, Judas,
Even the betrayer
His face tanned
By a golden halo
Turned in profile
And the thirteen auras
All at different heights
Bob and jostle above
The tablecloth's white Jordan
Like balloons, buoys,
Mooring lights...

In mid-channel
One full face
In solitude.

Nagasaki

CHRIST REJECTED

In the life of the ugly,
The plain, the lonely, sometimes
A stranger of great beauty comes
With an ease almost holy.

They who were never loved,
Who worshipped from afar with scorn
The beauty of the nobly-born
For a moment felt themselves moved.

How can it be? Who is he?
A stranger of great beauty,
With limbs perfect, smile all purity,
Comes, and gives his love to me?

It is as they tell us of
Jesus, loving the halt and the dumb,
Who, laying his hands upon lepers, did come
On earth, to give us of God's love.

How beautiful are thy feet with shoes.
The joints of thy thighs are as jewels,
The smell of thy nose like apples.
His legs are pillars of marble, his lips lilies...

The ugly believe, and know
That this is the love of Christ.
– But put an arm about the stranger's waist,
He melts away like snow.

The stranger of great beauty comes
And goes in lives that are plain,

Bringing love, but also fear; hope, but pain.
Ours are the hearts, but his the drums.

None can resist him, who are not
As perfect as he, but those sad fools
Who turn away as he comes with smiles,
And seek the comfort of the brothers he forgot.

SPACE CHILD SIGHTING REPORTED – DURING HEAVY BLIZZARD

Skidding down
On power lines,
Hovering in
His little craft,
Beaming in on us,
Then at the velocity
Of fright, flashing
Out of sight.

This was the boy
(Or girl) who came
This winter eve, on
Saturday night at the
Local, leaving nothing
But a blackened patch
At this touchdown in
The shepherds' field
Of snowy sheep, and
A couple of stunned
Beasts, an ox and an ass.

– This came to pass

B-29 MISSION

Death of an airman –
Tom Ferebee, aged 81 –
the *Enola Gay*.

He was in command
when the atom bomb was dropped
on Hiroshima.

He claimed neither he
nor his crew were told the bomb
was an atom bomb.

– 'It was not until
we returned to our airbase
that my general

asked what it looked like
from the air. Then I heard it
was an atom bomb.

From Guam, we sent
reports to the President –
to Harry Truman –

He praised the success
of our mission – two hundred
thousand or so dead

to the present day,
including those who had died
of radiation

and other sicknesses, long
after the bomb had dropped – the bomb
was an atom bomb.'

– Tom confessed all this
to Orlando journals in
nineteen eighty-five.

All those years, living
with the nightmare of that
crime – an atom bomb –

forty years of hell.
– And yet, he was not guilty.
Just another raid

and just another
B-29 mission. – May
his soul rest now in peace.

(From a report and obituary in *Le Monde* March 19th 2000)

IN MADRID – MARCH 11

haiku

Skies weep blood over
all the earth – and in Madrid
spring rain is falling

Heavy rain – millions
of hands clapping in protest
in the streets of Spain

Streets – canals flowing
with candlelight – with the tears
of millions of eyes